FROM THE EDITORS:

It's been a long and productive winter. For creative kind like ourselves it's the time to slow down, reflect and renew from within. We are lighting the way with our featured story and interview with Stephanie Reppas and looking forward to the next big thing that is already in the works!

Maxwell Alexander & Dino Alexander

© 2018 Hudson Valley Style Magazine
A Duncan Avenue Group Publication

Contact Us:
1-845-518-2750
Editors@HudsonValleyStyleMagazine.com
Advertise@HudsonVallleyStyleMagazine.com
Info@HudsonValleyStyleMagazine.com
Careers@HudsonValleyStyleMagazine.com

UNIQUELY
SOPHISTICATED
HOME
ACCENTS

MAXWELL
ALEXANDER HOME™

DUNCAN**AVENUE**.COM

5 DIY PROJECTS THAT WILL REINVENT YOUR BATHROOM IN A WEEKEND

(BPT)

Ready to tackle your next home remodeling project and showcase your Do-It-Yourself (DIY) skills? Or maybe you're an aspiring DIYer, hoping to channel your creative spirit and try your hand at the next home improvement project? Now is the time to get started.

According to experts from the National Association of Home Builders, the amount of money homeowners spend on remodeling projects is predicted to grow nearly 5 percent in 2018. Some of these dollars will be spent on large comprehensive rebuilds and others will be spent on smaller fix-it-up projects. No matter the spend, it's a good bet much of this money will go to fund DIYers in their home improvement efforts, and many of them will be taking on projects for the first time.

Here are five bathroom upgrade projects that can be completed in a weekend. So now you can reinvent your bathroom and employ your DIY skills at the same time. Go ahead, pick the project that appeals most to you, and let's get this project underway:

UPGRADE YOUR BATHROOM FIXTURES

The focal points of your bathroom can easily be replaced, making a big overall impact with little outlay of effort. Tapered design lines and modern styling, like those in the American Standard Townsend bathroom fixtures, can beautifully enhance your bathroom. Consider replacing an old vanity with a new smoked gray vanity or washstand. It can be accented with a softly angular sink displaying generously sized side ledges to conveniently accommodate toiletries. Finish the room with matching accessories - towel bars, toilet paper holder, robe hook - and you're on your way to a whole new level of style, all done with your DIY expertise.

INSTALL A NEW SHOWER DOOR

A shower door replacement can be made for cosmetic reasons; plus, there are very real potential benefits behind it as well, provided you pay attention to the details. Follow the process to install your door and be sure to apply silicone caulk at the end along the

↑ Sleek design lines and modern styling, like those highlighted in the American Standard StudioS faucets and Studio line of fixtures shown here, can beautifully enhance your bathroom to make it ideal for your family's needs.

edges of the base track - both inside and out - and along the jams. This will make your new door water tight and keep your whole bathroom cleaner and drier.

REPLACE YOUR SINK FAUCET

The faucet in your bathroom gets used every single day, so why not make it one you love? Ameri-

can Standard Studio S bathroom faucets showcase a fashion-forward geometric silhouette with minimalistic surface details. You can choose an easy-to-operate single handle model, or distinctive two-handle configurations, depending on what works for your home and family. These faucets are easy to install, and the WaterSense-certified 1.2 gallons per minute flow rate will save you water - up to 45 percent over conventional models - and money without compromising your experience.

LAY THE TILE

Whether you're motivated by structural needs or an outlet for your own artistic expression, laying new bathroom tile is a project that immediately ups the wow factor. Tile is incredibly impervious to water and stains, making it perfect for the bathroom. But it won't lay properly unless you thoroughly clean the surface beforehand. Fill those backboard seams with mortar, apply a fiberglass mesh and then you're ready to lay a tile design that matches your unique look.

A SPOT FOR THE PERFECT SEAT

If you've ever wished your time on the toilet seat was a little more luxurious, now is the perfect time to upgrade to an American Standard SpaLet bidet seat. It's easy to install and provides the ultimate personal experience with a wide array of features like heated seat, water temperature control, spray strength, nozzle position, and even a deodorizer. Now, you can bring a spa-like environment right to the comfort of your own bathroom, without much time or cost invested.

As one of the most used rooms in your home, the bathroom is the perfect place to start your weekend warrior home improvement projects. Simple upgrades to the elements in a bustling family bathroom, cozy master bath or heavy-use powder room can often be done with DIY know-how and enjoyed for many years to come.

↑ The focal points of your bathroom can easily be replaced to make a big overall impact with little outlay of effort, as shown here with the American Standard Townsend collection of bathroom fixtures and faucets.

LIGHTING THE WAY

*Exclusive Interview
by Maxwell Alexander*

*Lotus Pendant Light ↑
© Stephanie Reppas / October Design*

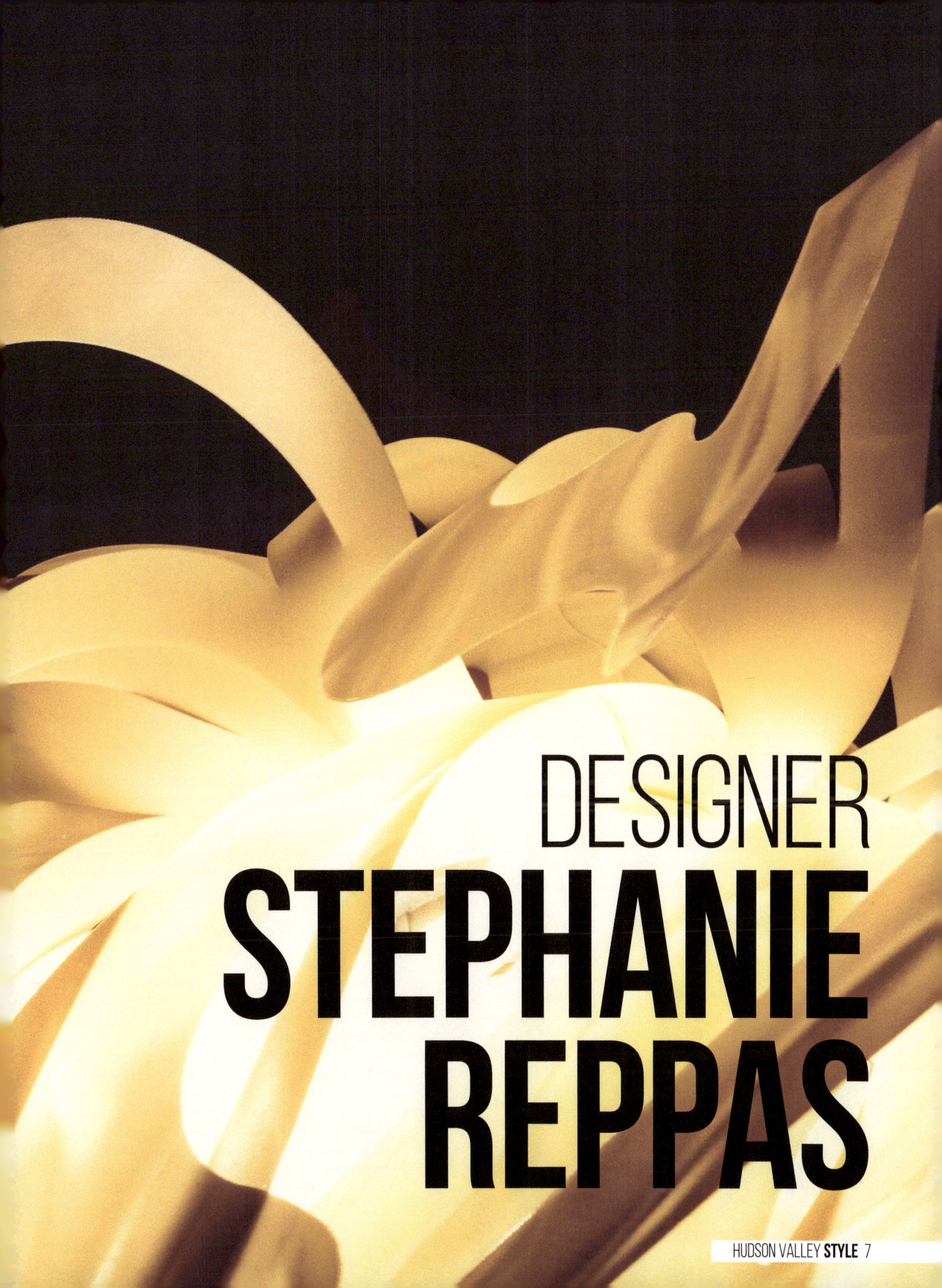

DESIGNER
STEPHANIE REPPAS

Max: Congratulations on the amazing cover shot, Stephanie! We are proud to have you lead the Winter Edition and shine the light on your beautiful work. When and how did Hudson Valley become your home, and how did you realize your lighting design talent?

Stephanie: I moved to the Hudson Valley in 2008. Before that, I lived in NYC, which was amazing, but after a few years I really missed having space and quiet. I'd read an article in The Times about the village of Sleepy Hollow. I was thrilled to learn that it was a real place (not just Washington Irving fiction) and it was located just 30 minutes north of Manhattan. I hopped a train up for a visit and was pleasantly surprised by the gorgeous ride along the Hudson River that passed through all of these wonderful little towns. Soon I found myself making frequent trips upstate to explore the different villages, until finally I realized I needed to move here and start a new chapter in my life. Hudson Valley just felt like home.

It's been the perfect environment for both my life and my business. I work primarily with reclaimed materials found around Upstate New York. I've always been attracted to the abandoned and obscure – finding value and beauty in things that others tend to overlook – and there's an abundance of both here. My first design was a Lotus pendant that I plasma-cut from a sheet of scrap metal. I originally intended for it to be a hanging sculpture, but once it was suspended in air, it seemed obvious that it should be outfitted with a light of some sort. Just like that, I was a lighting designer. A few classes in wiring and a degree in industrial design soon followed. I started pairing other objects I'd found with light, which added a whole new dimension and function to each design. Over the years, I've experimented with it more in an effort to create an intriguing play of shapes and shadows.

Max: I can relate to that! What are you working on at the moment and how does winter season in the Hudson Valley affect your creative workflow?

Stephanie: I tend to hibernate in the winter. Show season is over and things are quiet following the holidays, so I usually take January and February to regroup both personally and professionally. I tally everything I've accomplished in the past year and then plan the next twelve months. I'll research ideas, work out marketing and production schedules, develop new product lines, play with different design techniques and materials, maybe take a trip or two.

This winter, though, I have been fairly busy with a few custom and commercial installations: a polo club in California, an ice wine festival in Niagara, a spa in Woodstock, NY and the new Market & Cafe Co-op opening soon in Philmont, NY.

Max: What is the most favorite part of your design & creative process?

Stephanie: It's difficult to pick just one favorite. I've been very fortunate to be able to combine several of my passions into my work and my life:

I love traveling, exploring and the search for unusual industrial and rustic objects. They're always interesting, but they've typically been overlooked and under-loved. I think this kind of craftsmanship, which sometimes has lasted a century or more, deserves to be seen and reused, not just tossed and forgotten.

I love learning the stories behind the items I unearth: leather equestrian tack from a 200-year-old Amish settlement. Antique hand-carved sewing bobbins from an abandoned textile mill. Or 19th century glass photo negatives featuring a much-loved (and much-photographed) baby named Evelyn. The objects I salvage have weight, history and character.

I love the challenge of constantly working with different materials. My goal is to transform each object, while also working in a bit of whimsy with function.

And I love seeing people react to my designs, watching them light up and smile when they realize what a particular lamp or piece of furniture is made of. That's how I know I've done my job.

Max: What is your inspiration?

Stephanie: I like to stay open and experience as much as I can, but fundamentally I'm still attracted to just a few basics for inspiration:

Structured, industrial lines balanced by rustic, organic textures like distressed leather, exposed hardware, raw wood, chunky concrete and fibrous paper.

A neutral color palette: black, white, mocha, espresso, mushroom, stone, ash, silver.

Clean, minimalist design skewed by roughened, grungy edges.

Blurred, impressionist imagery.

Asymmetry.

Androgyny.

Nature.

"STRUCTURED, INDUSTRIAL LINES BALANCED BY RUSTIC, ORGANIC TEXTURES LIKE DISTRESSED LEATHER, EXPOSED HARDWARE, RAW WOOD, CHUNKY CONCRETE AND FIBROUS PAPER."

Egg Lamp ↑
(Salvaged Steel)
© Stephanie Reppas / October Design

And I have an exceptional community of friends: Artists, writers, photographers, comics, scientists, musicians, pilots, math whizzes, roller derby kings and queens. They're a smart, interesting and unconventional group of weirdos who bring creativity and weirdness out of me. They're the best inspiration!

Custom Birch Lamps →
© Stephanie Reppas
/ October Design

"ASYMMETRY.
ANDROGYNY.
NATURE."

Rivulet Mirror ↓
(Reclaimed Wood)
© Stephanie Reppas / October Design

Max: Is there an object in your own house that encapsulates Hudson Valley Style? If so, tell us the story behind it.

Stephanie: I have a beautiful vintage orchard ladder I found in Milbrook, NY a few years ago. It's weathered gray aspen wood and nicely ravaged by time and exposure to the outdoor elements. It's functional – I sometimes use it to hang my designs on while I work on them, but it's also a lovely décor piece and a design touchstone for me. I imagine it in its previous life sitting among apple trees, pumpkins, haystacks and fallen leaves in mid-October. It doesn't get much more "New York" than that!

"WHEN I MOVED TO THE **HUDSON VALLEY**, I KNEW THERE WAS **A FANTASTIC COMMUNITY OF TALENTED ARTISANS** HERE, AND I WANTED VERY MUCH TO BE A PART OF IT."

Max: Tell us more about how your Art became a successful business and where is it going next?

Stephanie: When I moved to the Hudson Valley, I knew there was a fantastic community of talented artisans here, and I wanted very much to be a part of it. It's great to see the same faces at shows and to be able to talk shop with others who are living the life and experiencing similar challenges. But I've also become a part of the even larger community of local business owners who are very gracious and invested in this area as well. They've made an effort to be here and are eager to bolster a sense of community by collaborating with other local businesses and regional artists. For example, the owner of GloSpa (Woodstock, NY) reached out to me this past winter. Her spa was in the middle of a remodel, and she felt strongly about featuring a local designer in her new salon space. She also appreciated that I use Hudson Valley-sourced materials in my designs. I created barber light fixtures and leather-framed mirrors to complement the beautiful new décor. It was great working with her, and I'm looking forward to popping by for a massage and facial this spring!

When I met the owner of Nine Pin Ciderworks (who is a Chatham resident), she had a very definite idea for a lighting installation for her new tasting room in Albany. She had some old cider barrels and IBC totes, and asked me to convert them into several quirky, oversized chandeliers. It was a very challenging project, and a collaborative one as well. I worked closely with a good friend, Michael Trezza, who helped me with cutting the barrels lengthwise, reinforcing the inner structure and securing the shape of the wood to incorporate industrial hanging hardware. No easy task, but the final fixtures look wonderful in the new space.

The villages here have a welcoming, close-knit community spirit to them, which I think makes it more attractive for others to visit Hudson Valley and want to be a part of it, too. And becoming a bigger part of this community is important for me as well. I've been surprised by my journey and how far I've come in just a few short years. My goal is to keep working, enjoy what I'm doing and hope it continues to amaze me!

Max: Thank you for shining the light, Stephanie! Literally :) We are looking forward to seeing more amazing Hudson Valley Style work from you and will be happy to have you back anytime!

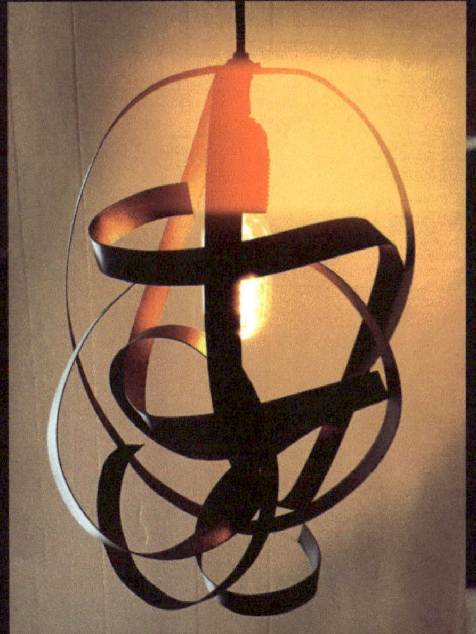

Scribble Lights ↑
(Made from salvaged duct strapping)
© Stephanie Reppas / October Design

Birch Bark Pendant Lights ↑ (Birch bark harvested
from downed trees)
© Stephanie Reppas / October Design

"The Evelyn" ↑ Pendant Light
(Antique Glass Negatives)
© Stephanie Reppas / October Design

SHOP **OCTOBER DESIGN CO.**

Vintage Barbicide Jar Pendant Lamp ↑
$105.00
octoberdesignco.com

Copper Funnel Pendant Light
$135.00
octoberdesignco.com

Equestrian Stirrup Table Lamp
$200.00
octoberdesignco.com

CREATING A DREAM HOME WITH CYPRESS

REACHING NEW HEIGHTS

Looking to add dimension and visual interest to otherwise flat, dull ceilings? Architect Geoff Chick of Santa Rosa Beach, Florida, says it's not enough to simply add crown molding. Too basic!

"Owners today are looking to celebrate their ceilings with more creative design solutions and materials," Chick says. "In large rooms where I have tall ceilings to work with, I typically use a coffered ceiling. Filling in the coffers with wood helps to warm up a room and add another layer of detail. Cypress with a square groove is my favorite wood to use for ceiling treatments. I just love how it looks, especially when combined with cypress beams."

(BPT) - Transforming the unremarkable into the extraordinary need not be an impossible task. More and more homeowners are finding that lavish looks are both attainable and affordable. Their imaginative design professionals are making it happen, using cypress to create their clients' dream homes.

"Wood is a classic and timeless building material," says Stephen Logue of the Southern Cypress Manufacturers Association. "And many people are discovering that the inherent beauty of cypress, a species so often chosen for outdoor applications, adds a luxurious look to indoor living spaces, for anything from walls and ceilings, to exposed beams and so much more."

Browse the Photo Gallery at www.CypressInfo.org and see how cypress transforms the unremarkable to the extraordinary. It's time to make your dream home a reality.

TRANSFORMING THE ORDINARY

When a coat of paint just won't do, think paneling. For Christopher Rose, an architect based in Johns Island, South Carolina, solid wood paneling provides a sense of warmth and richness to a room. But not just any wood.

"I particularly like working with cypress," says Rose. "It has a wonderful grain pattern that offers a relaxed, yet elegant look. Vertical beadboard or tongue-and-groove patterns are popular options that add perceived height to a room. And more recently, horizontal shiplap paneling and accent walls have been requested by many clients."

ADDING THE FINISHING TOUCH

When selecting a finish for his interior cypress woodwork, Chick prefers stains. "It's a shame to cover cypress with paint," Chick says. "To help bring out its grain pattern, I like finishing it with a matte stain or pickled finish. Some rooms require a lighter finish than others, and it can be a challenge to coordinate with flooring. But from my experience with cypress, it's all worth it when it comes together."

And remember, much like wood cabinets and floors, solid cypress paneling and ceilings can be refinished. If you're envisioning a fresh look down the road, swap neutral tones for bold colors, or sand the wood and apply a transparent stain to let cypress's natural beauty speak for itself.

ENCOURAGING

[AROMATHERAPY
MIST]

····· with ·····

BLACK SPRUCE
& SANDALWOOD
ESSENTIAL OILS

BLACK ROCK FOREST™

DA-AROMATHERAPY.COM

REAL ESTATE PHOTOGRAPHY 101

61%
MORE VIEWS ONLINE
WITH PROFESSIONAL PHOTOS

UP TO 
47%
HIGHER ASKING PRICE/SQFT

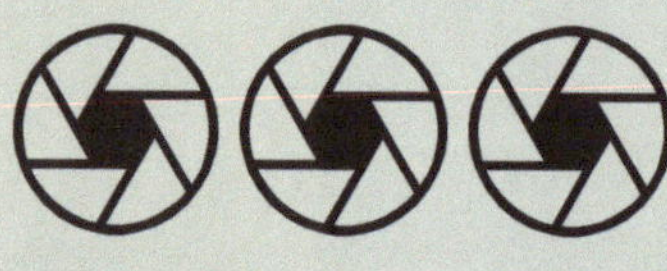

80%
OF BUYERS
CITED THEY WOULDN'T EVEN CONSIDER A LISTING WITHOUT PHOTOGRAPHS

98%
OF BUYERS
THINK PROFESSIONAL PHOTOS ARE MOST USEFUL WHEN LOOKING FOR HOME ONLINE

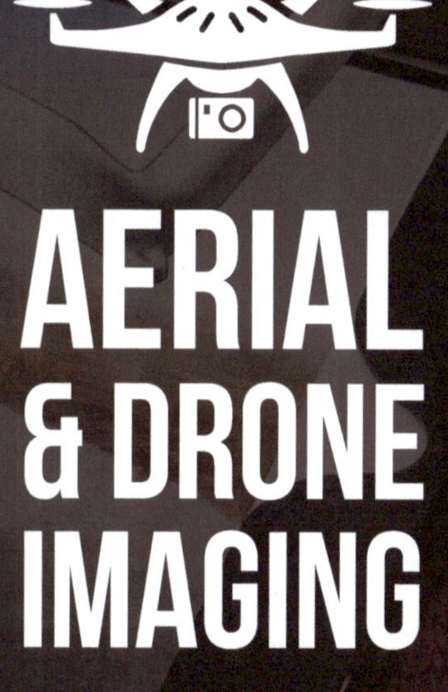

CONSIDER THESE HIGH-TECH UPGRADES

DUNCAN**AVENUE**™
HUDSON VALLEY REAL ESTATE SERVICES

SCHEDULE YOUR PHOTOSHOOT @
DUNCAN**AVENUE**.COM

STATISTICS SOURCE:
NATIONAL ASSOCIATION OF REALTORS

PROFESSIONAL LIGHTING

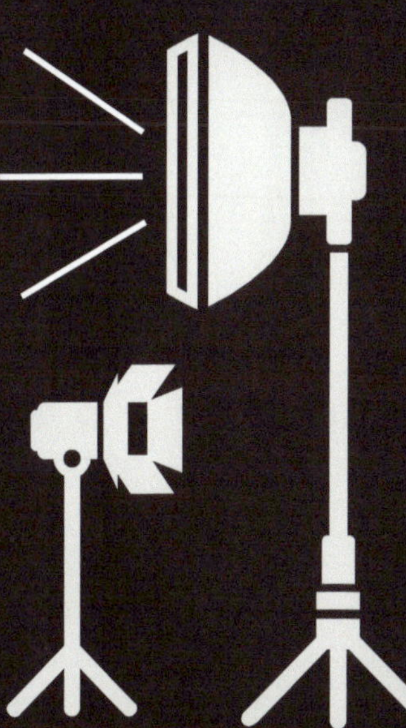

DSLR CAMERAS & LENSES

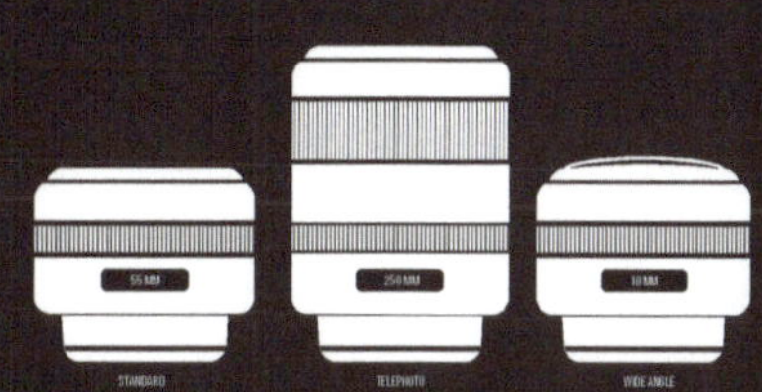

PROFESSIONAL RETOUCHING

+ DIGITAL STAGING

DA
AROMATHERAPY™
DA-AROMATHERAPY.COM

CREATE YOUR OWN CUSTOM AROMATHERAPY MIST
by DA Aromatherapy Collection

Create Your Own Natural Fragrance / Aromatherapy Mist with Organic Essential Oils! DA Aromatherapy Collection gives you the power to be your own natural fragrance & aromatherapy designer at your fingertips.

1. Select Your Top Notes
These are the first and most noticeable notes when you first smell the fragrance and include fresh, clean and sparkling citrus and herbaceous, grassy and minty essential oils.

2. Select Your Mid (or Heart) Notes
They open up your natural fragrance's true character, last longer, make a bigger impression and include floral, fruity and spicy essential oils.)

3. Select Your Base (or Dry Down) Notes
They are Earthy, Woodsy, Musky and ground your natural fragrance, balance it and make it last longer.

DA Aromatherapy Collection Essential Oil Mists is the easiest way to enjoy all the benefits of Aromatherapy on the go. Simply use it as your body mist or a refreshing room spray and lift up your mood any time and anywhere!

DA-AROMATHERAPY.COM

$17.00

INSPIRING AROMATHERAPY MIST WITH ORGANIC LAVENDER AND SANDALWOOD ESSENTIAL OILS - WINDS OF STORMKING™
by DA Aromatherapy Collection

A luxurious and sensual fragrance of rich, woodsy sandalwood accord and beautiful flowery notes of lavender and spice. Winds of Stormking™ Essential Oil Blend perfectly captures the cool mountain breezes, sun sparkles in the Hudson River waters and lush foliage of the Hudson Valley.

DA-AROMATHERAPY.COM

$9.00

NATURAL HAND SANITIZERS WITH ORGANIC ESSENTIAL OILS
by DA Aromatherapy Collection

Flu season is here! Protect yourself and loved ones and get aromatherapy boost on the go with these natural hand sanitizers. DA Aromatherapy Hand Sanitizing Mists with Organic Essential Oils are effective against 99.9% of common germs and bacteria.

DA-AROMATHERAPY.COM

$9.00

ESCAPE WITH 2018'S MOST IN-DEMAND COLOR
(BPT)
[STYLE & COLOR]
20 HUDSON VALLEY STYLE

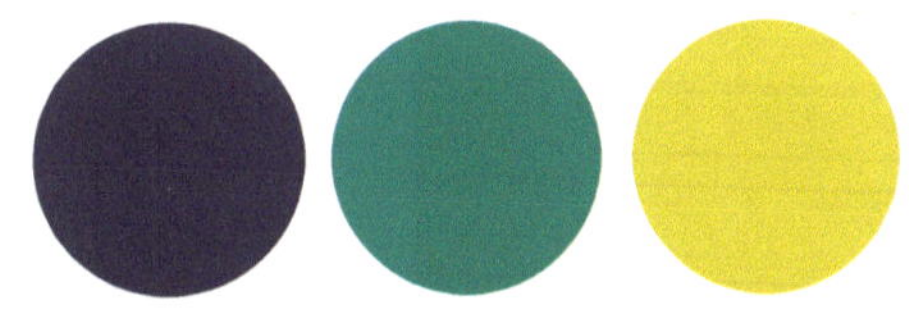

Whether you've been a loyalist to the same shade of green for the last decade or if you're an evolving follower of trends whose color choices have shifted over the years, the trending color of 2018 is sure to surprise and intrigue you. Indeed, black is back. But how was this classic shade named the trending color of the year? While many assume the choice is random, trending colors are based on many influencers, but where do they really begin? Trending colors arise from consumer preferences, which are formed by societal influences, such as politics, economics, lifestyle and overall sentiment. We as a society hold the power of prompting new color trends based on our ever-changing attitudes, ideas and actions.

Dee Schlotter, senior color marketing manager for PPG, a leader in paint and color, understands the path to determining each year's top trending color. Schlotter and more than 20 PPG color stylists from around the world meet annually at the company's Global Color Trends Workshop. "Our team of global color experts assess societal and cultural influences to forecast what colors will be popular in home decor, consumer goods, automotive and even airplanes for the upcoming year," Schlotter says. "We also look at what's happening in society, and the state of people's emotions because of current events. All of this information helps us predict what colors will truly resonate with people in the coming year, especially when it comes to the paint in their homes."

2018 finds its color of the year in a reflection of people's daily lives and their need to find an escape.

"BLACK" TO BASICS

"The PPG Paints brand's 2018 Color of the Year is Black Flame (PPG1043-7). It offers the silencing impact of black with the possibility and hopefulness of indigo seen in the color's undertone," says Schlotter.

Schlotter adds that black will be very popular in 2018 because it offers a break from an often chaotic and over-worked world.

"With society facing overstimulation and a need to take refuge, the color black offers a comforting retreat, and a chance to start new and get back to the basics," she says.

"Black Flame represents that necessary void and the need for nothingness that helps us recharge, making it a timeless and classic color in home decor."

A PALETTE OF OPTIONS

While going darker can seem intimidating at first, incorporating black into your existing decor is a lot easier than you think.

Many people mistakenly believe that all blacks are the same. However, black, like any other color, is available in a wide array of shades. For example, Glidden paint's 2018 Color of the Year, Deep Onyx (00NN 07/000), is a deep and rich black that encourages a less-is-more attitude when applying to home decor, while Black Magic (OL116), the 2018 Color of the Year for Olympic paints, is more glamorous and looks great as a statement color for walls. And, if you're looking for some darker inspiration outdoors, Olympic stain's Maximum product in a Cinder semi-transparent stain color (905) is a great complement to Black Magic when applied to exterior surfaces like doors, window trims and shutters.

Any of these black hues can be a defining piece in your decor while providing you with the mental escape you need. Schlotter adds that capitalizing on this year's color trend isn't solely about the color itself, but what you pair it with. Consider some of her other tips and tricks, including:

Pairing the PPG Paints brand's Black Flame with Millennial orange-pinks, teals and warm gray or mocha browns for an enveloping, rich look and feel.

Feeling a bit more daring? Make an impactful statement with black by applying it from floor to ceiling on an accent wall or in an entire room. Completing the look with lighter elements and furnishings will make the decor stand out, because the dark walls will highlight artwork and accessories while providing depth and character, creating a perfect space for respite and conversation.

To keep a space more fresh and modern, consider pairing a black hue with whites, matte finishes or light-grain wood finishes.

"Outside of paint, reinvented versions of the classic black hue are showing up in key design elements - from faucets, to matte black appliances, to black veined granite countertops, black windows and marble floors," says Schlotter.

"The possibilities are truly endless when it comes to adding this misunderstood neutral in the home."

It's your home's focal point. The site of some of your best moments and the base of operations for entertaining - it's your kitchen, and no room in your home is more valuable. A magnificent kitchen defines a home, and bringing your kitchen to this level means capitalizing on today's top trends.

Many of the trends that will define kitchens for the year appear first at KBIS, the kitchen and bath industry convention held every year in January. More than 600 brands attended this year's event, and here are the five trends that stood out from the show and are sure to dictate kitchen styles for the rest of this year and beyond.

APPLIANCES THAT CAN DO IT ALL

As home chefs have become much more refined, the need for kitchen appliances capable of delivering to these expectations has increased. Signature Kitchen Suite, the new-to-the-scene luxury brand, for example, debuted the first-of-its-kind pro-style range with built-in sous vide for the ultimate in precision cooking. The range is among the most versatile available with two extra-high burners that deliver 23,000 BTUs of cooking power and two ultra-low burners to maintain temperatures as low as 100 degrees. This appliance is also Wi-Fi enabled, which means you can monitor and control your kitchen wherever you are.

UNIQUE BACKSPLASHES

The tile backsplash still has plenty of staying power, but the latest trends are upping the wow factor of this kitchen mainstay. From mirrored glass and backlit onyx to decorative sculptures, the kitchen backsplash is becoming the statement piece of any kitchen and a unique way to express your own style and taste.

5 TOP TRENDS FOR YOUR KITCHEN IN 2018

(BPT)

MATTE BLACK FINISHES

The standard appearance of kitchen fixtures is taking on a darker tone in 2018, as matte black finishes are flourishing in a big way. This elegant, luxe appliance finish complements any kitchen and is also designed to conceal fingerprints and smudges. This smooth, low-gloss design option enhances any style kitchen, from modern to farmhouse, traditional to contemporary and every style in between.

DESIGN ELEMENTS

Long a place of functional purity, the kitchen is getting a dramatically artistic makeover in 2018. Designers from one side of KBIS to the other were showcasing lavish kitchens complemented with unique patterns, angles and texture choices. You simply wanted to go out and touch and savor every single detail they offered. The takeaway? It is possible to enjoy looking at your kitchen as much as you enjoy working in it.

SMARTER KITCHENS

New Wi-Fi enabled appliances are helping people control their homes in new ways, allowing for greater convenience - either through the touch of a button on their smartphone or via voice commands through Amazon Alexa and Google Assistant. Want to preheat the oven before you head home from work? Done! Need a fresh batch of ice before company arrives? You don't even have to get up. Forget to turn on the dishwasher? No problem. Choose a cycle and turn it on from virtually anywhere. Smart home leaders like LG have also teamed with food and recipe services such as Innit and SideChef to better assist home chefs with planning, shopping, preparing and cooking delicious meals.

Taking your kitchen to the next level The latest and greatest innovations for your kitchen were on display at KBIS, but bringing them home is up to you. Need more renovation inspiration? Check out new virtual design tools to experiment with different styles and appliance combinations to create your dream kitchen. You may just find a whole new look for your kitchen.

CUT EXPENSES WITHOUT CUTTING CORNERS ON YOUR BATHROOM REMODEL

(BPT) - When homeowners get the urge to remodel and renovate their homes, two rooms immediately top the list: the kitchen and the bathroom. In the last decade, we've seen something of a renaissance in home bathroom design. From an innovative use of materials to radically reimagined bathtubs and toilets, today's bathrooms offer a dream space with comfort and convenience in a stylish package.

This dream, however, comes with a price tag. A mid-range bathroom remodel that includes a steel tub, a pressure-balanced shower, ceramic tile floor, vanity and integral sink could cost almost $20,000, and that's for a 5-by-7 room. An upscale remodel might cost as much as $60,000!

But before this sticker shock scares you away, know there are secrets to saving money and still getting a beautiful bathroom. We sat down with Lynn Schrage, interior designer at Kohler Co. to learn some of her tips and tricks. Here are five of the best.

1. FIND A FOCAL POINT

You don't need to have top-of-the-line everything to create a stunning bathroom. Think in terms of what piece you want to be the star of your bathroom. Maybe you want it to be the sink, a freestanding bathtub or a spa steam shower. Pick one fixture that will draw the eye in and take center stage. You'll be amazed at what this does for the overall effect.

2. INCORPORATE CREATIVE STORAGE SOLUTIONS

In remodeling a bathroom, it's always exciting to stumble upon a solution that brings together the practical and the beautiful. This happens a lot when you try to figure out how to store toiletries, towels and more. Wall cabinets, wicker baskets, storage ladders and storage towers create charm and keep your essentials orderly.

3. A TOUCH OF LUXURY GOES A LONG WAY

One of the most effective ways to create a stunning overall effect is to mix a touch of luxury with quality materials. For instance, coordinate wooden cabinets with a tiled paneling treatment around the bathroom. Also ripe for coordination are choreograph shower panels with stone or porcelain tiles. Focusing and investing in these luxury elements while using quality material will help offset costs and give you the look you've dreamed of.

4. SELECT AN INTEGRATED VANITY TOP SINK

Looking through your many choices of sinks, showerheads, toilets and other fixtures is downright inspiring, but sometimes it can be hard to know where to start. Of all the options available, consider setting your eye on a vanity top with sink mounted on any number of vanity styles you like. This combines style with functionality in a timeless design and cuts down on clean up and your installation cost.

5. WORK WITH A PROFESSIONAL

Many people who want to save on a bathroom remodel think the most economical way is to go it alone and take the DIY route. However, a professional designer can help you discover the style that fits your personality and budget - and help you avoid costly mistakes. For instance, Kohler's Bathroom Design Service provides expert advice, 3-D bathroom renderings and logistical guidance.

To discover more inspiration for your bathroom, visit ideas.kohler.com, where you'll find the ideas and advice that will get you started on your journey to your dream bathroom.

WHY IT IS A GREAT IDEA TO STAGE A HOUSE BEFORE SELLING IT

By Dino Alexander (New York State Licensed Real Estate Broker)

Want to sell your home quickly and for top dollar? Staging can help. Staging is presenting your home in its best and most appealing light to the majority of home-buyers.

In theory, staging isn't hard or costly, but in reality, many homeowners find it difficult because it's often hard to see something objectively when we love it.

An easy way to see effectively staged homes is to visit decorated models. Decorating a model is expensive, but builders are willing to invest the cost because they understand just how well a staged home sells. You too can profit from this knowledge.

Why do some sellers balk at staging their home? They think it's too expensive, they think it's too much work, they like their decorating, and they don't understand the value.

Expensive? No nearly as much as your first price reduction.

Work? Mostly cleaning and de-cluttering which you would have to do anyway since you're moving.

Decorating? Liking your decorating is understandable. Look at it this way – interior design is for living in your home, staging is for selling your home. They are distinctly different.

Value? Okay, there's the catch. How much does it really do for me?

WHY IT IS IMPORTANT TO STAGE A HOUSE BEFORE SELLING IT:

- Get the Highest Price for Your Home. A well-staged home is aesthetically pleasing. Everything looks inviting, comfortable, and simple. It elicits a strong emotion from buyers: desire.

- Your Home Will Sell Faster – The Association of Property Scene Designers states that staged homes sell for 43% more quickly than unstaged homes.

- Staging Helps with Procrastination – yes, your stager will want many of your collector items put away. This is called de-cluttering and depersonalizing. You will have to tackle this at some point. Get it done early, store boxes in the basement, a POD, or rent a storage unit for a few months.

- Staging will teach you a Few Things. Maybe you never had a decorator and you've done it all yourself. Those floral curtains in the bedroom, the layout of the pictures over the living room sofa, the furniture placement in the family room or the overlarge chair in the den. It all works for you which is great – but a stager might just show you "better" which is something you can take with you to your new home.

- You Never Get a Second Chance to Make a First Impression – is a favorite line with stagers and real estate agents. If you don't stage before you list, guess what? You've lost time and money – the two things that are all but promised if you stage your home before listing it for sale.

- You get a good feeling when you walk into a home that has been properly staged. It's not fake, it's more than just place mats and wine glasses on the dining room table. It just feels good.

TO STAGE, OR NOT TO STAGE?

STAGED HOMES SELL 79% FASTER

STAGED HOMES SOLD IN 11 DAYS OR LESS
COMPARED TO AVERAGE 90 DAYS ON THE MARKET
ON AVERAGE SPEND 73% LESS TIME ON THE MARKET

81% OF BUYERS FIND THAT STAGING HELPS THEM BETTER VISUALIZE A PROPERTY AS THEIR FUTURE HOME

HIGHER SALES PRICES
STAGED HOMES SELL FOR 17% MORE
THAN NON-STAGED HOMES

BUYERS MOST OFTEN offer 1%-5% increase on the REAL VALUE OF A STAGED HOME

SELLERS SPEND LESS THAN 1% FOR STAGING SERVICES to get a 1000% RETURN ON INVESTMENT

HOME STAGING CAN BOOST PERCEIVED VALUE OF A HOME BY 20%

95% OF BUYER'S AGENTS SAY THAT HOME STAGING HAS A POSITIVE EFFECT ON THE HOME BUYER'S VIEW OF THE PROPERTY

3% YET LESS THAN 3% OF HOMES LISTED ON MLS ARE STAGED

DUNCANAVENUE™
HUDSON VALLEY REAL ESTATE SERVICES

SCHEDULE YOUR CONSULTATION @
DUNCANAVENUE.COM

STATISTICS SOURCE:
NATIONAL ASSOCIATION OF REALTORS

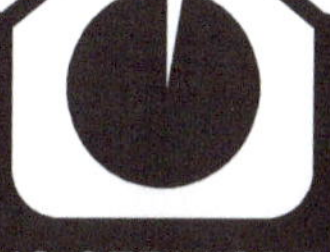

EXPERIENCE THE MAGIC OF HUDSON VALLEY™

PLANT DERIVED INGREDIENTS / NO PARABENS
NO SULFATES / NO DEA/MEA VOC-FREE / BIODEGRADABLE
CRUELTY-FREE / GOOD FOR YOU & GOOD FOR
THE ENVIRONMENT / MADE IN THE USA / DESIGNED &
CRAFTED IN HUDSON VALLEY

DA-AROMATHERAPY.COM

HUDSON VALLEY
[STYLE]
MAGAZINE
ADVERTISE.
HUDSON VALLEY STYLE.
INFO@HUDSONVALLEYSTYLEMAGAZINE.COM

TURN YOUR BASIC BACKYARD INTO AN OUTDOOR OASIS

(BPT) - Summer is around the corner, but are you ready to make the most of it? Creating a vibrant outdoor space can expand the living area of your home, while providing a unique venue for entertaining or relaxation, allowing you to enjoy every free moment to the fullest.

From the ultimate sports bar to a zen paradise, the outdoor design possibilities are endless and can be customized to meet your priorities, be it entertaining friends and family or creating the perfect tranquil retreat. As a leader in home comfort for nearly 40 years, Napoleon has extensive expertise in designing products and environments that help create memorable moments that last a lifetime. The company recently enlisted a third-party research firm to help examine the connection people have to different areas of their home and outdoor spaces, and how the design of those spaces can have a direct impact on emotions.

"The research shows the most-loved areas of the home combine relaxation, socialization and functionality," said Stephen Schroeter, Napoleon's senior vice president of sales and marketing. *"Outdoor spaces provide a great opportunity to accommodate all three, yet they are still vastly underutilized by most homeowners."*

Following are Schroeter's top tips for creating the outdoor oasis of your dreams:

1. ADD AN OUTDOOR KITCHEN

- Outdoor kitchens are growing in popularity, and for good reason. Not only do they meet a basic need, but they do so in a fun, engaging atmosphere. No one wants to be stuck inside preparing a meal when the party is out under the sun - or stars. The showpiece of every great outdoor kitchen is a quality, professional grill, which can be freestanding, or built-in to save on space. Napoleon's Prestige PRO Series grills are packed with features for professional-level grilling right in your own backyard. Innovative products like the OASIS Outdoor Kitchen allow you

to personalize your outdoor area with a cooking and storage solution that fits your space and your budget. Other culinary considerations include outdoor refrigerators or beer dispensers to keep beverages cold and flowing freely, pizza ovens and sinks for easy clean-up.

2. ESTABLISH A GATHERING PLACE

- One of the most important features of an outdoor space are areas for socialization. A central location with a variety of seating options creates a welcoming atmosphere. Adding the element of fire to a space sparks emotion, provides a focal point, and enables the space to be used later into the season. Consider a built-in fireplace or a fire pit that can be moved to different locations depending on your needs.

3. CREATE PRIVACY, DIVIDED ZONES

- Escape the hustle and bustle while making your space feel more intimate with the use of barriers like large plants or trees, a pergola, or privacy panels. Designing distinct spaces with divided zones helps create the feel of a secluded getaway and gives each area purpose.

4. Design for all the senses - Our favorite spaces are those that delight all the senses. In addition to designing a comfortable, beautiful space, consider adding outdoor speakers for music that sets the mood, or a water feature that eliminates street noise. Relax and enjoy the delicious smell of grilling or the experience of roasting marshmallows over an open flame. Consider adding fragrant bushes to fill the night with a sweet scent. Get creative.

5. ADD ACCENTS

- Small touches can go a long way. Personalize your space with items that define your style and personality or focus on a fun theme. Don't be afraid to add bold pops of color - your outdoor living area is a great place to explore a more adventurous design than you might consider inside your home.

It's never too late to transform your backyard into a welcoming oasis. For more outdoor design ideas, visit http://napoleonfireplaces.com/inspiration/outdoor-spaces.

DA
AROMATHERAPY™
SOOTHING
AROMATHERAPY
MIST
with
EUCALYPTUS
& PEPPERMINT
ESSENTIAL OILS
2 FL. OZ. // 59 ML.
CALMING
AROMATHERAPY
MIST
with
LAVENDER
& CHAMOMILE
ESSENTIAL OILS
2 FL. OZ. / 59 ML.

SCROLL LESS. BREATHE DEEPER.
DA-AROMATHERAPY.COM

5 SMART TECHNOLOGY UPGRADES

TO MAKE THE BATHROOM THE BRAINIEST ROOM IN THE HOUSE

(BPT) - Smart technology has found a place in virtually every room in the home, even the one where we take care of our most low-tech needs. In fact, thanks to innovations like sensor-operated, self-cleaning toilets, moisture-sensing ventilation fans and digital shower controls, it's possible to turn an ordinary bathroom into the brainiest room in the house.

If you're ready to upgrade your bathroom with the latest smart technology, here are five elements to put at the top of your must-have list:

1. SMARTER SHOWER

From showerheads with light and sound, to digital temperature and water pressure controls that you can set from your smartphone, an array of high-tech features is available to elevate the simple act of getting clean to the level of a luxurious, high-tech experience.

You can find something for every preference. Love to shower at night? Install a showerhead that features its own lighting. Dislike fiddling with the controls every morning to get just the right temperature? Opt for digital temperature controls that allow for multiple pre-settings for individual users. Focused on conservation? Try a showerhead that senses what you're doing - washing your hair, shaving your legs - and automatically adjusts the water flow accordingly.

2. INTELLIGENT TOILET

A toilet that cleans itself is a dream come true for many people, but TOTO boosts the intelligence of its NEOREST AC wall-mount toilet even higher. The intelligent toilet features a WASHLET personal cleansing system that uses warm, aerated water for comfort, a warm air dryer and a heated seat. An automatic opening and closing function and auto-flush ensure you never have to touch the toilet.

The toilet keeps itself (and the environment in your bathroom) clean with a flushing system that uses an environmentally friendly combination of gravity and high-speed water jets to spin away waste, while an in-bowl catalytic deodorizer helps keep the air fresh. The bowl itself is glazed with titanium dioxide and zirconium, which when activated by the toilet's integrated UV light, creates molecular reactions that help keep the bowl free from visible and invisible waste.

Not only will you not need harsh detergents to clean the toilet, it's is also WaterSense labelled, and uses just 1.28 gallons per flush (gpf) for solid waste and 0.9 gpf for liquid. Visit www.totousa.com to learn more.

3. VERSATILE VENTILATION

Bathroom ventilation fans serve practical and cosmetic purposes. Ventilation removes moisture and humidity that could promote the growth of mold and mildew, and can help exhaust unpleasant odors. Of course, not everyone puts ventilation to its optimum use, and that's where a new style of bathroom fan comes in.

Ventilation fans that sense humidity - such as after someone has taken a long, hot shower - turn on automatically to help remove excess moisture from the room. Some fans can communicate wirelessly with wall switches or with an app that allows you to control the fan from your smartphone.

4. MULTI-TASKING MIRROR

Mirrors and medicine cabinets aren't just for reflection anymore. Now you can kit out your smart bathroom with mirrors that feature built-in TVs and can communicate with your home's security cameras, and medicine cabinets with defogging features that can let you get to your post-shower shave faster.

Refrigerated medicine cabinets are perfect for preserving delicate drugs and cosmetics, and you can find both mirrors and medicine cabinets with built-in USB ports for charging your devices.

5. ADVANCED ACCESSORIES

Of course accessories can be additions that put any bathroom over the top, and you never have to settle for ordinary accessories in your smarter bathroom. Enhance the usability and convenience of your bathroom with items like:

A SMALL ROBOT THAT MOPS FLOOR TILES AUTOMATICALLY.

A BLUETOOTH-ENABLED TOOTHBRUSH THAT COMMUNICATES WITH YOUR SMARTPHONE

DIY. STAGING TIPS

1. CLEAN.

Your home must sparkle! To achieve this level is often only feasible by hiring a cleaning crew. In fact, having a cleaning service return weekly while your house is for sale is probably a pretty good investment. Get your windows professionally cleaned inside and out too.

2. FIX.

Got a dripping faucet or a cracked tile? These will send the wrong message to potential buyers. Getting them fixed before you put your house on the market is a smart idea.

3. DE-CLUTTER.

The "50% Rule" requires that you eliminate the clutter in your home by at least half. We love our clutter – it reflects our memories, hobbies, and values. But it doesn't sell homes! Clutter makes homes seem smaller and disorganized. (Have you ever noticed that the really expensive stores seem to have an expansive, clutter-free layout, while "cheap" stores are often a jumble of merchandise?)

4.

GO PASTEL.

Pastel colors sell. It's a fact. Try to convey an image of quality and neutrality. Potential buyers walking through your home want to imagine themselves as the owners. If you use bold styles or colors they would never select, you've just turned them off. Staying high-quality, contemporary & classy with neutral shades of grey.

5.

DE-PERSONALIZE.

Remove objects that your potential buyers won't be able to identify with. For example, political and religious items may turn off whole groups of buyers, because they cannot "imagine" your home as their home. Buying a home is an emotional decision, and you want potential buyers to make an emotional connection with your home by being able to "see" themselves in it.

[DIY STYLE]

Sara Golden

SARAGOLDEN.COM

UNIQUE HOME ACCENTS

MAXWELL ALEXANDER | HOME™

aglaïa

Recycled metal is as beautiful and timeless as newly mined and indistinguishable in its use as a raw material, Aglaia Jewelry made its choice, did you?

aglaiajewelry.com

DA AROMATHERAPY NATURAL
HAND SANITIZERS
DA AROMATHERAPY
COLLECTION BY DUNCANAVENUE
MADE IN USA
NATURALLY DERIVED ESSENTIAL OILS
DESIGNED & CRAFTED IN HUDSON VALLEY
DA-AROMATHERAPY.COM

THE BEAUTY OF BARN DOORS

(BPT)

The master bath in a Dallas house ↑ by Modern Craft Construction features a barn door and accent wall both made of walnut. Photograph by RUDA Photography.

BARN DOORS MOVED OUT OF THE FARMYARD AND INTO THE HOUSE A LONG TIME AGO. RECENTLY, HOWEVER, THEY HAVE BECOME AN EVEN MORE POPULAR AND USEFUL FEATURE IN RESIDENTIAL DESIGN. IT'S NOT HARD TO SEE WHY.

"Many homeowners hear the term 'barn door' and think of reclaimed, rustic wood, which may not be a look they're interested in," says Linda Jovanovich of the American Hardwood Information Center. "But contemporary barn doors offer many more aesthetic choices than their traditional image suggests. We've noticed a trend toward the use of solid, fine-milled hardwoods like walnut and cherry for sliding doors, which not only gives them satisfying heft but is also a great way to bring the warmth and character of natural wood into an interior."

New York-based interior designer Laura Bohn agrees. "I've installed hardwood barn doors in many projects, both in the city and the country," she says. "They provide a lot of decorative interest, particularly hung in pairs. I'd choose a clean, sophisticated design in a subtle wood like maple or birch for an urban interior. Poplar planks painted a cheerful color, or characterful woods like hickory and cypress would be better for doors in a country house."

Along with their decorative qualities, barn doors often provide a functional alternative to conventional swing doors. "Barn doors, either singly or in pairs, offer a simple and effective way to divide large spaces - a kitchen from a living-dining area, for example," says Laguna Beach, California-based designer Lisa McDennon. "They can create instant separation and privacy in even the most open-plan house, which allows for greater flexibility in daily use."

"A traditional door can use up to nine square feet of space, which is a lot in city apartments where every inch counts," notes New York-based designer Glenn Gissler. "A barn door only takes up a sliver of floor, making it a terrific solution in tight situations such as hallways and narrow rooms. You just need enough adjacent wall footage to slide the door over."

Barn doors offer economic advantages, too. While pocket doors have similar space-saving benefits, installing them requires wall reconstruction - a messy and expensive business. Because barn doors run on hardware installed outside the frame, they need no such preparatory construction, saving time and money. And the tracks themselves are part of the doors' decorative appeal. "There's a terrific selection of barn-door hardware available," Bohn says. "Use sleek, high-tech tracks in brushed aluminum or satin-finish stainless steel for a modern urban vibe. For a more rustic or industrial statement, think blackened iron or raw steel, both of which look powerfully graphic against natural or painted wood."

Visit www.hardwoodinfo.com for more about residential design trends and other applications and products using American hardwoods.

SEE WHAT'S NEW
@DUNCANAVENUE.COM
DA
PROPERTIES

DO THE MATH: HOMEBUYING NOW MAY SAVE A LOT

IT IS A COMMON MISCONCEPTION THAT A 20 PERCENT DOWN PAYMENT IS REQUIRED TO BUY A HOME.

Advice to wait and save a large down payment is often based on the theory that the cost of mortgage insurance (MI), which is required when you buy with a smaller down payment, should be avoided. This may not be the best advice and is, in fact, not in line with market trends, considering 60 percent of homebuyers buy with a down payment of 6 percent or less, according to the National Association of Realtors.

YES, YOU CAN QUALIFY FOR A CONVENTIONAL MORTGAGE WITH A DOWN PAYMENT AS SMALL AS 3 PERCENT OF THE PURCHASE PRICE.

It is also true that you can reduce your monthly mortgage payment by paying for discount points at closing, but that can be 5 or 10 percent of the purchase price - not 20. And because every buyer's situation is unique, it's important to do the math. In today's market, it could take a family earning the national median income up to 20 years to save 20 percent, according to calculations by U.S. Mortgage Insurers using a methodology developed by the Center for Responsible Lending; a lot can change during that time, in the family's personal finances and in overall mortgage market trends.

HOW CAN BUYING NOW SAVE YOU MONEY LATER?

Consider you want to purchase a $235,000 home. A 5 percent down payment is $11,750 versus $47,000 in cash for 20 percent down. With a 740 credit score at today's MI rates, your monthly MI payment would be about $110, which is added to your monthly mortgage payment until MI cancels. MI typically cancels after five years; therefore, you will only have this added cost for a short period of time versus waiting an average of 20 years to save for 20 percent.

WITH HOME PRICE APPRECIATION, TODAY'S $235,000 HOME WILL LIKELY

COST MORE IN THE YEARS AHEAD AND THIS WILL ALSO HAVE AN IMPACT ON THE NECESSARY DOWN PAYMENT AND LENGTH OF TIME REQUIRED TO SAVE FOR IT.

There are other variables in the equation too, such as interest rates. As federal rates rise, so too can the costs associated with financing a mortgage. The savings a borrower might calculate today could be altogether negated by waiting even a few more years. Another factor is that rents are on the rise across the nation, leading to a reduced capacity for many would-be homebuyers to save for larger down payments.

If you decide to buy today with a low down payment mortgage option, it is true that MI is an added cost on top of mortgage principal and interest, but keep in mind that it is temporary and goes away.

Again, it typically lasts about five years.

Private MI can be cancelled once a homeowner builds approximately 20 percent equity in the home through payments or appreciation and automatically terminates for most borrowers once he or she reaches 22 percent equity. And when MI is cancelled, the monthly bill goes down. Importantly, the insurance premiums on an FHA mortgage - the 100 percent taxpayer-backed government version of mortgage insurance - cannot be cancelled for the vast majority of borrowers with FHA mortgages.

SO, DO THE MATH AND LET THE NUMBERS GUIDE YOU. THERE ARE MANY ONLINE MORTGAGE CALCULATORS THAT CAN HELP.

Check out lowdownpaymentfacts.org to learn more.

WINTER: TIME TO GET READY FOR SPRING

By Bria Tavakoli
briayoga.com

Are your new year's resolutions now a distant memory? Did the simple thought of them cause you to cringe?

Let's be honest. Some of us feel an intense internal resistance to new year's resolutions, then feel bad when our resolutions and good intentions fizzle out or even flop. I'm here to tell ya...there are natural reasons why we feel this resistance.

Before we continue here, let me state that if you are into new year's resolutions, I support you. Do you, do what works. Personally, I'm not into new year's resolutions because they feel out of sync with the actual season. Before writing me off as lazy and in need of a nap (though that might be slightly true), hear me out. In many cultures, including the Persian culture of my heritage, the new year is actually the first day of SPRING. Not January 1!

Winter is the season of going inward. Our bodies and souls crave it. Those of us who live or even play in the Hudson Valley get to experience all four seasons, and their inherent wisdom, fully. I teach yoga in the city, and almost every New Yorker I have spoken to in recent weeks is feeling the urge to sleep more, eat more (carbs, I'm lookin at YOU!), and to do more home-bodied type things, anything from watching movies to cooking to meditating. Luckily, the Hudson Valley lends itself to both indoor and outdoor rejuvenation.

IT'S ONLY NATURAL. SUCH INTERNAL REJUVENATION OF THINGS WINTER IS MADE FOR. HIBERNATION. RELAXATION. REFLECTING. RE-GROUNDING. SNOW DAYS, SNOW ANGELS!

This slowing down is generally a good sign. As Ayurveda (a holistic health system developed thousands of years ago in SE Asia) would corroborate, this is your body and soul being in tune with nature. Whether we live in the Hudson Valley countryside, in town, in a concrete jungle or somewhere in between, we are all a part of nature. We sometimes forget that, but it's true.

Back to resolutions: Thinking we are going to re-invent ourselves or our lives during this time of year starts to really look and feel counter-intuitive, considering we may well be better off supporting and nurturing ourselves in preparation for oncoming growth.

For example, think of plants. Seeds need time underground in the cool, moist earth to hydrate, assimilate nutrients, and prepare to sprout. Then it takes a lot of energy to germinate and sprout. That cannot happen without the right amount of light, darkness, sun, food, and water. And stillness. It just cannot.

So why the heck do we expect ourselves to blossom when we're feeling drained and exhausted to start with?

Trying to revamp in a huge way this time of year is like running with the cold wind blowing at your face, rather than having the refreshing spring wind at your back, pushing you along. Winter wind's adding unpleasant, unnecessary effort and pressure to your life. Rest, reflection, and patience will get you to a time and place when you could move into changes with more support, joy, and ease. Yes, like Mama always said, "Sometimes to get there fast, you gotta go slow."

And yet a lot of my yoga students and friends feel BAD, downright guilty about this intuitive desire to downshift. I say ditch the guilt. Know that this time of year is custom-made for us to downshift. I'd go so far to say that our future success depends on it. Rebooting now, plus embracing steady, consistent progress rather than over-reaching for giant overhauls, will open us up for productivity, growth, and creativity as we move towards spring and summer.

SO WHAT DOES THAT LOOK LIKE DURING THIS TIME OF YEAR? YOU COULD USE THE TIME TO:

- Reflect
- Journal
- Get clarity on what you want in your life going forward (Ask yourself this life changer: What do you want, not what society or others say you should want!)
- Meditate (guided meditation practices like Yoga Nidra absolutely count!)
- Sleep earlier, and longer
- Snuggle and nap more (my kitty loves it when I am on point with my kitty nap game)
- Take a pass on extraneous obligations
- Go slow and steady with any new routines or reboots (Now is not the time to push your yoga or gym routine to the max, for example; it's a perfect time for slow, steady progress)
- Eat grounding foods like potatoes, beans, nuts
- Spend quality time with your dear ones
- Get up early to get a few extra minutes of sunlight in your day (especially if the lack of light darkens your mood; this is easier to do when we sleep earlier ;-))
- Plan a getaway. One idea: join my spring mind-body retreat weekend in the Hudson Valley, April 20–22, 2018.

Yes, winter can be a dark time for a lot of us: literally and figuratively. If we use the darkness as a chance to reflect and rejuvenate, we can find that very darkness quite supportive, rejuvenating, and illuminating.

LUXURY REAL ESTATE
IN HUDSON VALLEY

AM ALEXANDER MAXWELL REALTY™

ALMAXREALTY.COM
info@almaxrealty.com
1-845-518-2750

www.ingramcontent.com/pod-product-compliance
Lightning Source LLC
Chambersburg PA
CBHW040139240726
48664CB00002B/545